contents

Dúchas The Heritage Service

An Roinn Ealaíon, Oidhreachta, Gaeltachta agus Oileán
Department of Arts, Heritage, Gaeltacht and the Islands

© 2000

introduction

Rising above the flat fertile plain of the River Suir in the heart of the old province of Munster, the Rock of Cashel or St Patrick's Rock must always have been an impressive feature of the landscape. Today, the buildings which crown the Rock, present a mass and outline of great interest and beauty unequalled in these islands.

Once the seat and symbol of the overkings of Munster, this naturally defensive fortress was given to the Church in 1101 and, soon after, became the seat of an archbishop. Gradually the secular fortress was submerged beneath ecclesiastical structures. The oldest of these, the round tower, probably dates from around 1101. Next in age is Cormac's Chapel, the finest Romanesque church in Ireland, which was consecrated in 1134. Squeezed between these is the massive 13th-century cathedral, the towers of which were added later. Lastly the 15th-century range of buildings, now restored, was the domestic quarters of the Vicars Choral. Also of great interest are a stone cross and sarcophagus from the 12th century and tomb sculpture from the 13th to 17th centuries.

It was as a fortress that the Rock of Cashel first came to prominence and aptly the name itself (*caiseal* in modern Irish) is an early borrowing from the Latin *castellum* (a fort). Its origins as a centre of power go back to about the 4th or 5th century AD when the Eóganacht, the descendants of a legendary Eógan Mór, son of Ailill Ólum, first appear on the scene. No written history relating to Cashel survives from this early period, only legends that were committed to writing much later. Conall Corc, a descendant of Eógan Mór, was said to be the founder of the Cashel kingship and the stories associated with him suggest that he may have been a returned Irish settler or mercenary from Roman Britain. The first Irish converts to Christianity may also have been in Munster and traditionally a number of its saints, such as Ailbe of Emly, were claimed to have pre-dated St Patrick. It appears that the Cashel kingship had Christian associations from the start. In contrast, the other provincial royal centres, Cruachain in Connacht, Dún Ailinne in Leinster, Emain Macha (Navan Fort) in Ulster and Tara in Meath, were important pre-Christian burial and ritual centres of great antiquity.

However, a late 7th-century life of St Patrick claims, almost as an afterthought, that he baptised the sons of Nio Froích, son of Conall Corc on Patrick's Rock at Cashel. A later version has the story that during the baptism the saint's sharply pointed crozier pierced the foot of Óengus mac Nad Froích, who, believing it to be an essential part of the ceremony, suffered in silence.

The main importance of Cashel in the early historic period was as the seat and symbol of the overkingship of Munster and as the inauguration place of its kings. Eóganacht dynasties were spread throughout Munster and, up to the 10th century, only Eóganacht kings were eligible for the Cashel kingship. In this period two great overkingships emerged in Ireland: the Eóganacht kingship of Cashel, often controlling most of the southern half of the country, and the Uí Néill kingship of Tara, claiming hegemony over the northern half. Both groups began to covet an overkingship of all Ireland. Certainly Cashel kings like Cathal mac Finguine (713-42) and Fedelmid mac Crimthainn (820-47) posed a serious threat to the Uí Néill kings of Tara.

The Rock from the north-east.

history

An unusual feature of the Cashel kingship is that a number of its kings were also ecclesiastics. Though Fedelmid mac Crimthainn was also a bishop it did not prevent him raiding church property in other territories. Cormac mac Cuilennáin, who became king of Cashel in 902, was a renowned scholar as well as a bishop and compiled a famous glossary, the text of which survives. His serious challenge to Flann Sinna, king of Tara, led finally to his own defeat and death at the battle of Belach Mugna (Ballaghmoon, Co. Kildare) in 908, a defeat from which the Eóganacht never fully recovered. By the later 10th century the kings of Dál Cais, centred around Killaloe in Co. Clare, ousted the Eóganacht from the Cashel kingship. Brian Boraimhe (Boru) of the Dál Cais succeeded his brother as king of Cashel in 978 and went on to become the most powerful king in Ireland. He became king of Tara in 1002, the first Munster king to achieve the high kingship of Ireland. He was killed at the battle of Clontarf in 1014. A saga about Brian claims that he fortified Cashel and his great grandson Muircheartach Ua Briain had a residence there in 1091.

In 1101 Muircheartach Ua Briain, king of Cashel and contender for the high kingship of Ireland, was to change the history of Cashel forever. At a synod he convened there, he 'made a gift to religion that no king had ever given before him, that is to say, he gave Cashel of the Kings to the clergy'. By this masterstroke he both advanced his credentials as a church reformer and simultaneously deprived his old enemies, the Eóganacht, of their ancient royal seat. At another synod patronised by Muircheartach in 1111 at Rath Breasail (near Glankeen, Co. Tipperary), Ireland was for the first time divided into territorial dioceses with archbishops at Armagh and Cashel. It was not until the synod of Kells in 1152 that official approval arrived from Rome for the archbishoprics, by which stage four rather than two were approved, Tuam and Dublin having been added. This system of dioceses has remained largely unchanged to the present day.

After Muircheartach's death in 1119 a branch of the Eóganacht, surnamed Mac Cárthaigh and based in

Desmond (South Munster), regained a measure of power and influence at Cashel. This resulted in Cormac Mac Cárthaigh, king of Desmond, building the beautiful Cormac's Chapel there between 1127 and 1134. Recent excavations indicate the existence of a small church and burial ground at the site dating from about the 9th century, possibly associated with those kings who were also ecclesiastics. Cashel would be expected to have had a relatively large church or cathedral soon after 1101 and certainly by 1111. This would have been associated with the round tower and probably stood on the site of the east end of the 13th-century cathedral choir.

At the invitation of Diarmuid Mac Murchada, a small army of Anglo-Normans arrived in Ireland in 1169 to assist him in regaining the provincial kingship of Leinster. Their leader, Strongbow, was promised Diarmuid's daughter Aoife in marriage and the succession to the kingship of Leinster. They were so successful in reconquering Leinster along with the key towns of Wexford, Waterford and Dublin that the king of England, Henry II, became concerned about his subjects setting up a rival Anglo-Norman kingdom in Ireland. He therefore came to Ireland in the winter of 1171 to lay claim to the conquests. Both the king of Desmond and Domhnall Mór Ua Briain, king of Thomond (North Munster) submitted to him at or near Waterford. Early in 1172 Henry convened a synod at Cashel which was attended by most of the Irish hierarchy.

It has often been stated that Domhnall Mór Ua Briain built a cathedral at Cashel in 1169. There is, however, no reliable evidence for this and it is possible that an early 12th-century cathedral continued in use until the surviving 13th-century Gothic building was constructed. No records relating to this 13th-century construction survive so that the evidence for its dating is purely

history

architectural. The east end or choir was probably begun under Archbishop Marianus Ua Briain (1224-38) or his immediate successor David mac Cellaig Ó Gilla Pátraic, who died in 1253 and who founded the Dominican Friary in the town. The rest of the cathedral was probably completed during the long episcopate of David Mac Carwill (1253-89) who also founded the Cistercian abbey of Hore to the west of the Rock.

According to the 17th-century historian, James Ware, Archbishop Richard O'Hedian (1406-40) endowed the Vicars Choral with lands and built a hall for their accommodation on the Rock. The cathedral was greatly altered in the 15th century, possibly also by O'Hedian, in that the parapets and crossing tower were added and maybe the residential tower at the west end. According to the 16th-century historian, Stanyhurst, the cathedral was on one occasion in the 1490s burned by Gearóid Mór, Earl of Kildare, who excused himself to Henry VII as follows:

'By Jesus I woulde never have done it, had it not bin
tolde me that the Archbishoppe was within'.

This burning, if indeed it ever took place, does not appear to have been very destructive.

The Reformation initially had relatively little effect at Cashel and Edmund Butler was left in place as archbishop until his death in 1551. His successor, Roland Baron or Fitzgerald, appointed by the Catholic Queen Mary was also recognised by the Pope. After his death in 1561 rival archbishops were appointed by both the Crown and the Pope, the former, however, holding possession of all official Church property including the Rock. In 1571 Queen Elizabeth appointed Miler Magrath as archbishop of Cashel, a position he continued to hold until his death at the age of 100 in 1622. Miler started his church career as a poor Franciscan friar and was made Catholic bishop of Down in 1565. He became a Protestant by accepting

Reconstruction of the Rock in the 15th century

history

royal supremacy in 1567 and was rewarded with the see of Clogher in 1570 and Cashel in the following year. At various times he held other dioceses along with Cashel and up to seventy livings. He married twice, was the subject of a long condemnatory poem in Irish but may have been reconciled to Rome on his deathbed. His tomb, with an intriguing Latin inscription of his own composition, survives in the cathedral (see section on the choir). In marked contrast to him was Dermot O'Hurley, appointed Catholic archbishop of Cashel in 1581 and executed in Dublin three years later.

As a result of the 1641 rebellion, the Rock came into Catholic hands but witnessed harrowing scenes of bloodshed in 1647 when it was besieged by Murrough O'Brien, Lord Inchiquin, on behalf of the English parliament. As well as the garrison of Confederate Catholic troops, the townspeople had also sought refuge within the enclosure. When it was eventually stormed and captured by Inchiquin there followed a great slaughter of lay people and clerics. According to a contemporary witness, Fr. Andrew Sall: 'The large crucifix that towered above the entrance to the choir had its head, hands and feet struck off, the organ was broken, and the bells, whose chimes cheered our soldiers as they fought, were deprived of their clappers and their beautiful tone... All the passages, even the altars, chapels, sacristies, bell-tower steps, and seats were so thickly covered with corpses, that one could not walk a step without treading on a dead body'. Soon after, the Catholics regained control of the damaged cathedral. Evidence for this is a chalice which was made for use there in 1649, the very year that Cromwell arrived in Ireland to initiate the complete reconquest of the country for the English parliament. To avoid further bloodshed, Cashel surrendered to him and Cromwell made his headquarters there for a time.

It is likely that further damage occurred before Protestant worship resumed in the cathedral and there are records of repairs being carried out in the later 17th century. In the early 18th century Cormac's Chapel was used as a chapter house and the croft above served as a schoolroom. Archbishop Bolton carried out some further restoration in 1730 but during the term of his successor Arthur Price (1744-52) approval was given by the government to abandon the old site and confer cathedral status on St John's Church in the town. The old cathedral on the Rock remained partly roofed for some time and Archbishop Whitcombe was installed in both cathedrals in 1752.

It gradually fell into decay and Archdeacon Cotton, writing in 1848, described the accumulation of the debris of the roof within the building and the collapse of part of the residential tower in that same year. Also most of the east gable of the choir fell during these years of abandonment and neglect. When the Protestant Church of Ireland was disestablished in 1869 it was decided that important ecclesiastical ruins should be taken into State Care as National Monuments. The Office of Public Works was given the task of caring for these monuments. The Rock of Cashel was the first monument at which works were undertaken, between 1874 and 1876, under the supervision of the newly appointed Inspector of National Monuments, Thomas Newenham Deane.

In 1975, the Hall of the Vicars Choral was reroofed and restored. Its undercroft became a display area for stone sculpture including the original St. Patrick's Cross, which was replaced by a replica on the old location outdoors. The dormitory of the Vicars Choral to the east was excavated and restored in the 1980s and now houses an audio-visual theatre and offices. Most recently a long campaign of conservation has been completed on Cormac's Chapel including the frescoes in the chancel. The site is now managed and conserved by Dúchas the Heritage Service of the Department of Arts, Heritage, Gaeltacht and the Islands.

A print of the Rock from Ledwich's Antiquities of Ireland, based on an original by Charnley dating from about 1750.

site map

A. Entrance
B. Hall of Vicars Choral
C. Dormitory of Vicars Choral
D. St. Patrick's Cross (Replica)
E. Cormac's Chapel
F. The Cathedral
G. Round Tower
H. Enclosing walls &
   corner tower

Section through choir & elevation
(as redrawn by H.G. Leask, c.1940)

ground plan of cathedral

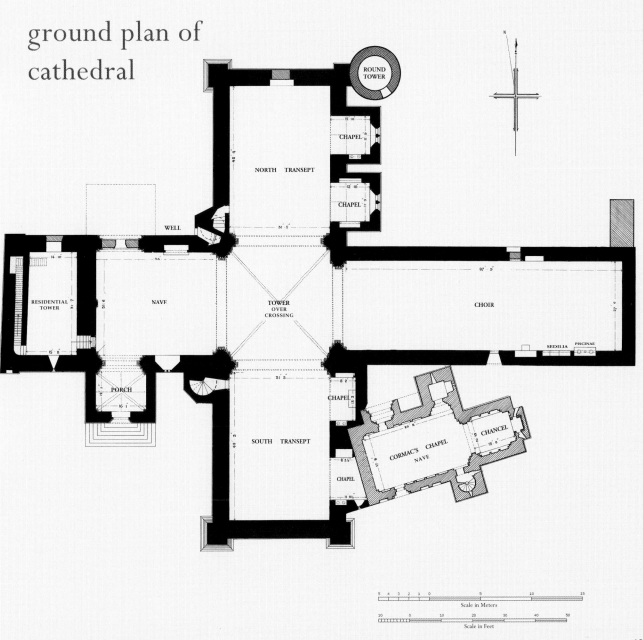

ROUND TOWER

N

CHAPEL

CHAPEL

NORTH TRANSEPT

WELL

RESIDENTIAL TOWER

NAVE

TOWER OVER CROSSING

CHOIR

SEDILIA   PISCINAE

PORCH

SOUTH TRANSEPT

CHAPEL

CHAPEL

CORMAC'S CHAPEL NAVE

CHANCEL

Scale in Meters

Scale in Feet

site description

St Patrick's Cross

Between the Hall of the Vicars Choral and the cathedral is a replica of the 12th-century cross (the original is on display in the undercroft of the Vicars Choral). St Patrick's Cross is unusual among Irish high crosses in not having a ring around the cross head and in having had subsidiary supports at each side of the shaft although only one survives. In keeping with most of the 12th-century or late high crosses there is a figure of the crucified Christ on one side clad in a full-length robe. On the other side is a large figure of a bishop or abbot. It has been argued that the prominence given to figures of bishops on these crosses is associated with the reform of the church at that time and the establishment of territorial dioceses in which Cashel played a major part.

Traces of decoration can be seen on the large stone base: an interlace pattern with birds on the east face, a repeating pattern of recessed crosses on the south face and sixteen concentric circles or a spiral with an uncertain motif at the centre on the north face. The often-repeated suggestion that the base was the inauguration stone of the kings of Cashel is highly improbable, the stone having clearly been chosen, quarried and worked along with the cross itself for its present purpose. An archaeological excavation of the site, after the cross was moved to the Hall of the Vicars Choral, showed that this was not its original location which is likely to have been somewhere on the site of the 13th-century cathedral, the building of which necessitated its removal.

St. Patrick's Cross

Cormac's Chapel

Until the arrival of the Romanesque style in Ireland in the early 12th century, Irish stone churches were plain rectangular structures with little or no stone carving. Cormac's Chapel, probably one of the very earliest churches in Ireland in this new style, is also one of the finest, most complete and ornate. Cormac Mac Cárthaigh, king of Desmond (South Munster) began the building in 1127 and the completed structure was consecrated in 1134. The novel features, which have parallels in England and on the continent, include the string courses and blind arcading on the internal and external walls, the multi ordered doorways with carved tympana, (the stones which fill the inner semicircular heads of arches), the rib-vaulted interiors and the towers and spiral stairs. It has been suggested that in turn Cormac's Chapel influenced other Romanesque churches in Munster such as Roscrea, Co. Tipperary and Ardfert and Kilmalkedar in Co. Kerry though none of these is built entirely of squared sandstone blocks like Cashel.

The building consists of a nave and chancel with a projecting tower at the east end of both the north and south walls of the nave. The nave also has opposing doorways in its north and south walls and both nave and chancel have connecting attic chambers (crofts) above their rib-vaulted ceilings within the space of their steeply pitched stone roofs.

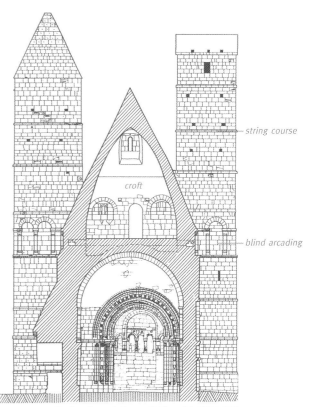

string course

croft

blind arcading

Section through Cormac's Chapel looking east

South transept of the cathedral and Cormac's Chapel

site description

The approach to the building from the south clearly shows the finely cut sandstone facade with its blind arcading, string courses and doorway, its projecting south tower and steeply pitched stone roof. The arched doorway is of three orders and has an animal carved on the tympanum. This is not as impressive as the original main entrance, a larger, more ornate and imposing doorway on the north side of the building. This is now partly buried in the walls of the Gothic cathedral and faces into a dark, damp corner hemmed in between the chapel and the walls of the cathedral. It would originally have faced onto an open space to the west of an earlier smaller cathedral (on the site of the east end of the gothic choir). The outer part of this north doorway forms a porch with a stone gable above it carved with chevron (zigzag) designs and rosettes. It has a very fine tympanum carved with a large lion being hunted by a small centaur (half man, half horse) with a bow and arrow and a Norman-type helmet. To the left of the doorway and under the same stone roof as the porch is an external recess probably designed to serve as a founder's tomb.

The interior of the nave has blind arcading on its walls and the flat lower pillars are decorated with a variety of designs. Above is a barrel or plain round vault with ribs. The nave was originally lit only from the west by three windows now partly blocked and obscured externally by the transept of the later cathedral. Towards the east end of the nave are archways in the north and south walls leading to the towers. That to the south is a small doorway leading to a spiral stairs within the tower, which gives access to the crofts above. The larger more ornate arch in the north wall gives access to the ground-floor room of the north tower, which appears to have been a tiny subsidiary chapel and has traces of painting on its walls.

A puzzling and unusual feature of the chapel is the fact that the chancel is positioned off-centre to the nave. The chancel arch, of four orders, has finely carved pillars and capitals and arch orders with chevron designs and roll mouldings. The second order from the outside has a remarkable series of stone heads on the pillars and arch. Some of these appear to have different racial or cultural characteristics and might have been intended to represent the different peoples of the world. The roll mouldings in the arch retain a considerable amount of their original 12th-century decorative paintwork of ornate roundels and scrolls.

Fresco on chancel ceiling   *Chancel arch capitals showing four orders*

The chancel itself is almost square in plan with an externally projecting altar recess at its east end lit by narrow windows in its sides. The side walls of the chancel have blind arcading with one of the arches on the south side framing a window opening. The two ribs of the vault above the chancel spring from the corners and cross at the centre, dividing the under surface of the vault into four triangular areas. All, including the ribs themselves, have traces of fresco painting. The western

site description

triangular area has considerable remains of a scene with three figures beneath painted arches. The suggestion has been made that the richly attired male and female figures beneath the larger painted arch are Solomon and the Queen of Sheba with a depiction of the temple of Jerusalem in the top corner. Single unidentified figures beneath arches can be seen flanking the rib at the springing of the vault in the southwest corner. There are extensive remains of paintwork on the south wall including part of a scene depicting the baptism of Christ in the arch to the east of the window and lattice patterns within the lower arcade. Two layers of painting, both very early in the building's history, have been identified on the walls. Much of the colour was obscured for many years by dirt and whitewash and is only now visible after painstaking cleaning and conservation work carried out as part of a major conservation project on the building in the 1980s and 1990s. In Irish medieval churches, surviving mural paintings are very rare and these examples are the earliest and some of the most complete to have survived. The quality and range of pigments used, including vermilion and lapis lazuli, is very impressive with different shades of the colours being achieved. Clearly it was an expensive undertaking with certain ingredients having had to be imported from the Orient.

Archaeological excavations in 1992-3 revealed the postholes of a small wooden church beneath the chancel of Cormac's Chapel and associated burials to the north of it. This wooden church, which was rebuilt once, stood for some time and might even have gone out of use before being replaced by a much larger stone structure to the north, presumably the forerunner of the present ruined cathedral. Burial continued in this area up to and after the time Cormac's Chapel was built. The excavation was important in establishing the existence of a church at the site from as early as the 9th or 10th century.

The Sarcophagus

At the west end of the nave of Cormac's Chapel is an ornate stone sarcophagus (coffin) which, though roughly contemporary with the chapel itself, was not directly associated with it. When first noted in the early 19th century it was then in the south chapel of the north transept of the 13th-century cathedral and was only moved to its present location in 1875.

The partly damaged front panel of the sarcophagus is carved in false relief with intertwined beasts and snakes in a manner strongly influenced by the Scandinavian Urnes style. This style first appears in Ireland around 1100 and though the sarcophagus is often claimed as the tomb of Cormac himself it is more likely to be that of his brother and predecessor as king of Desmond, Tadhg, who died in 1124 'after penance at Cashel'. Like the chapel, this sarcophagus is also unique in Ireland. Other stone sarcophagi, such as the example in the hall of the Vicars Choral, date from the 13th/14th century.

site description

The Cathedral

The cathedral is a large cruciform Gothic church without aisles. A tower, built in the 15th century rises from the crossing between the main east/west axis of the church and the north and south transepts. About the same time, a large residential tower was constructed at the west end of the cathedral. Crudely fitted in between three earlier features: the round tower, Cormac's Chapel and a rock-cut well now beneath the spiral stairs at the north-west pier of the crossing, the cathedral is also on a significantly different alignment to Cormac's Chapel. Despite these constraints the cathedral, built over a number of decades from about 1230 to 1290 is an interesting and imposing structure. One of its glories is the extensive and varied collection of stone heads used on capitals, label stops and corbels both inside and outside the building. One can imagine these representing churchmen, kings, lords, ladies, merchants and labourers; some poker-faced, some smiling, others grimacing. Many are high above the ground and difficult to see without suitable light and binoculars.

The Choir

To the east of the crossing is the choir of the cathedral, at the east end of which the high altar would have been located. Closer to the crossing there would have been rows of wooden choir stalls ranged against the side walls. Only the lower part of the east gable, with the lower section of its three-light east window, now survives. The series of tall lancets (pointed windows) at the east end of the south wall and west end of the north wall are in keeping with a building date of around the 1230s. High up, between the tops of these windows, are small quatrefoil windows in larger splayed openings. The original carved stone in the choir is of sandstone in contrast with the limestone used for fine carving in the later part of the building to the west.

Interior of the cathedral from the south entrance

A blocked-up doorway in the north wall, which led to an attached sacristy or chantry chapel, no longer surviving, has an unusually intricate design of roll moulding on its pointed arch. To the right of this doorway is the arched wall tomb of the Protestant Archbishop Malcolm Hamilton (1623-9), the inscription on which, according to Harris, was entirely erased during the reign of James II 'by some ignorant papist'.

Laid on the ground in this area is a collection of grave slabs mostly of the 16th century, with 7-armed segmented crosses and inscriptions in black-letter or gothic script. The family names represented are Archdeacon, Boyton, Butler, Cantwell, Comyn, Connery, Conran, Hackett, Hayden, Kearney, Meagher and Sall. The people commemorated in this fashion were usually either merchants of the town, church officials or local landowners. In the south-east corner is the lower part of a slab with an incised figure (feet only) dating from the 13th or 14th century.

In the south wall, starting at the east end, are the piscina (a niche with a stone basin and

Windows in the choir

drain, where the sacred vessels were washed), the damaged sedilia (where the celebrants sat at certain points during Mass) and the wall tomb of the notorious Miler Magrath, who was Protestant archbishop of Cashel from 1570 to 1622 (see history section). This is an arched recess containing an effigy of the archbishop, armorial bearings and a lightly incised figure of St Patrick below a plaque containing a Latin epitaph in raised lettering. This has been translated by Harris as follows:

The ode of Miler Magrath, Archbishop of Cashel, to the passer-by.

Patrick, the glory of our Isle and Gown,
First sat a Bishop in the See of Down.
I wish that I, succeeding him in place
As Bishop, had an equal share of Grace.
I served thee, England, fifty years in Jars,
And pleas'd thy Princes in the midst of Wars;
Here where I'm plac'd I'm not; and thus the Case is,
I'm not in both, yet am in both the Places

He that judgeth me is the Lord. 1. Cor. 4. 1621
Let him who stands, take care lest he fall.

The work is signed by the sculptor Patrick Kerin. To the west of this tomb is an inserted doorway, which led to a chamber or sacristy, built in post-medieval times between the choir and the chancel of Cormac's Chapel.

site description

Pier of the crossing and transept chapel

The Nave

The nave or west arm of the church is unusually short, especially in comparison with the considerably longer choir. In most churches and cathedrals the nave is longer than the chancel or choir. It seems that the 13th century plan envisaged at least a slightly longer nave with the north and south doorways placed midway along it. The residential tower, built about the 15th century, takes up the whole west end of the original nave and clearly involved almost the total rebuilding of the walls as if the original had collapsed or had never been fully completed. Opening off the residential tower was a first-floor hall accommodated within the upper part of the nave and two rooms with fireplaces above the porch.

The porch with its groin-vaulted ceiling is the main entrance to the building. An intended matching porch on the north side no longer survives and, apart from a smaller doorway, its inner arch is blocked. In the south wall of the nave to the east of the entrance is a window, which has been partly converted into a tomb niche. It contains an inscribed slab of the O'Kearny family and remains of early 17th century stucco (ornate plaster work) on its side walls and head. On the left are the remains of a crucifixion, on the right a coat of arms and on the head a centre-piece with four angels surrounded by the sun, moon and stars. Set in a niche in the north wall of the nave is an interesting plaque with a coat of arms and the inscription 'LAUS DEO 1574 SCUTUM SALL' (Praise to God 1574 The shield of Sall). The Sall or Saul family, originally of Norman origin, were prominent merchants in Cashel and beneath the shield is a rare example of a merchant's mark flanked by the letters E and K, possibly the first initials of one of the Salls and his wife.

17th-century stucco

Sall armorial plaque

site description

The Transepts and Crossing

The impressive arches of the crossing are original 13th-century work and rise from clustered banded columns with ornate capitals. The plainly ribbed vault in the centre was mostly reconstructed in 1875 having, according to tradition, been damaged when the bells were removed after the 1647 siege. It appears that the original design did not include a stone crossing tower. The present tower and the parapets at the tops of the walls date from the remodelling of the cathedral in the 15th century.

The side panel from a 16th-century altar tomb with carvings of the following: St. Brigid with a cross-staff and the following apostles: Philip with loaves in a cloth; Bartholomew with a knife; Matthew with a long axe; Simon holding a model ship; Thaddeus with a club and Matthias with a long knife. Five of the figures also carry a book.

The end walls of both transepts contain large three-light windows, which were lowered in height in the 15th century. The spiral stairways in the angles between the transepts and the nave give access to passages in the walls of the transepts. These run through the high bases of the windows and rise above the arches of the transept chapels to give access, through a doorway above the arch leading to the choir, to the space above the crossing vault. The passage in the north transept also leads to the round tower by a doorway broken through its west wall.

Opening off the east side of the north transept are two chapels, each having an east gable with a two-light window. In the area of the north transept are some fine examples of 16th century tomb sculpture including side and end panels from table tombs with apostles, other saints, a crucifixion and coats of arms. Set against a blocked doorway at the north end of the transept is a side panel with niches filled with very fine foliage and animals. There are traces of painted plaster on the walls of the transepts and choir.

The chapels in the south transept are far shallower because the pre-existing Cormac's Chapel allowed no scope for their extension eastwards. As on the north side, there is a statue niche in the wall between the chapels. In the south chapel a tomb side with a crucifixion, St Peter (with the keys of heaven) and a bishop (either St Patrick or St Thomas à Becket) is displayed. The west window of Cormac's Chapel opens into this chapel.

The Exterior of the Cathedral

Immediately west of Cormac's Chapel, the south gable of the south transept is an imposing piece of Irish 13th-century architecture in the Gothic style. Corner piers with fine canopied statue niches flank the three tall lancet windows, which were shortened in the 15th century. The statues have long since disappeared but the carved heads on each side of the niches are worth examining. Octagonal turrets with pyramidal tops crown these corner piers.

The stairs turret in the angle between the transept and the nave is mostly of 13th-century date. It gives access to the wall tops and also now to the 15th-century crossing tower. Further west is the porch with steps leading up to it. Its outer doorway is a 15th-century insertion. The residential tower to the left lost most of its south wall in a storm in 1848 and a displaced chunk of masonry still lies where it fell on the ground to the south.

Left: Transepts and crossing. Above: Choir windows.

site description

A smaller stair projection can be seen in the angle between the north transept and the nave. Beneath it and approached from the outside is a short passage containing a well-shaft. This rock-cut well is over 8m deep and predates the cathedral. It may be the only visible trace of the pre-1101 royal fortress.

The gable end of the north transept is similar to that of the south transept with its windows and corner piers with canopied niches. Only the central quatrefoil of the rose window over the three lancets is now open. The rest may have been blocked in the 15th century, when the tall lancets were shortened, possibly to save money on glazing. However, the outlines of the original windows were retained and not altered completely as happened in the Dominican Friary and Hore Abbey. Near the boundary wall to the north east, stand two 19th-century mausoleums of the Scully family. An extremely tall 19th-century carved stone cross stood on top of one of these until it was damaged in a storm in the 1970s.

The Round Tower

The round tower which abuts the north-east corner of the north transept is the oldest surviving building on the Rock. Round towers were free-standing bell towers built between the late 10th and the mid-12th centuries and unique in their shape and form to Ireland. Mostly they are found only at important ecclesiastical sites and their doorway often faces towards the west doorway of the principal church at the site.

The round tower at Cashel (28m high) is a particularly fine example, complete right up to its conical stone roof. It was faced with irregularly coursed wrought limestone and sandstone. There are small putlog holes in the facing for securing the scaffolding during construction. Its round-headed doorway is well above ground level, a common feature among round towers, and faces south-east presumably towards the west doorway of the main church then on the site. It originally would have had wooden

floors connected by ladder. The intermediate floors are lit by small lintelled windows while the top floor, which housed the bell or bells, has four evenly spaced triangular-headed windows.

The only historically dated round tower in Ireland is that at Clonmacnoise, Co. Offaly, which according to the annals was completed in 1124 by the abbot and the king of Connacht. The tower at Cashel may be slightly earlier and could have been built by Muircheartach Ua Briain to mark the handover of the Rock to the Church in 1101. This is well within the long radiocarbon date range of 880-1260 determined from mortar samples taken from the tower.

The Hall of the Vicars Choral

To the south of the cathedral, and forming part of its enclosure at the head of the steeply inclined approach road to the site is a long two-storey building. In the early 15th century, Archbishop O'Hedian first built the hall and, slightly later, the dormitory to the east, to house the Vicars Choral, a group of men, both lay and cleric, appointed to sing during the cathedral services. At Cashel there were originally eight vicars who were granted lands for their upkeep. Collectively, they had a seal as a corporate body.

The upper level comprises the hall or main living room of the Vicars with a large secondary fireplace in its south wall. The inscription on it reads: 'E.S. ET E.H. ME FIERI FE[CERUNT]', indicating that two individuals with the initials E.S. and E.H. (possibly a Sall and a Hayden or Hackett) had the fireplace made. This room has been restored with a timber gallery at its west end. All of the carved oak in the gallery and the roof is the work of modern craftsmen as is the timber medallion over the fireplace, which is based on the seal of the Vicars Choral. The vaulted undercroft beneath the hall contains a collection of stone sculpture mostly from the Rock. The original St Patrick's Cross is housed here to protect it from weather damage. To the right of the cross is a damaged late 13th-century effigy of a layman on its own stone sarcophagus, which is decorated on one side with small quatrefoils between pointed arches. This came from the site of the Franciscan friary in the town. Attached to the south wall is an unusual side panel from a 13th-century tomb with armoured knights in niches. This piece is from Athassel Priory and is carved in Dundry stone from quarries near Bristol in England.

At the west end of the room are fine carvings of an elephant and castle, damaged side panels from a tomb, depicting the four evangelists and a depiction of two griffins in high relief. Along the north wall are a caryatid figure, with no arms and entwined legs, from a 17th-century wall tomb and a number of coats of arms carved in stone. Both the hall and the dormitory have typical 15th-century windows with ogee heads. A sheela-na-gig (an exhibitionist female figure), contemporary with the building, is carved in a horizontal position on the corner of the dormitory, as indicated below.

The hall and dormitory of the Vicars Choral from the south

Sheela-na-gig

Artefacts associated with the Rock

One of the oldest finds from the site is a Roman type fibula or brooch. This was found between the cathedral and Cormac's Chapel during conservation works in the 1870s. It dates from the later 1st century AD and is now in the National Museum of Ireland.

Probably the best known object found on the Rock is an enamelled bronze crozier-head of 13th-century date which was made at Limoges in France and is now also in the National Museum. The head is of scroll type, the hook itself being formed of a serpent enclosing the figures of St Michael and the dragon. It was found about 1766, apparently in a stone coffin within the cathedral.

A large bronze hand bell in the Hunt Museum in Limerick is known as the Cashel Bell because it was found near the town of Cashel in 1849. It has finely incised ringed crosses on its main faces and is likely to date from around the 9th century. In 1988, a bronze bell-crest was recovered from soil on the floor of the croft above Cormac's Chapel. It is the handle of a bronze hand bell and is decorated with animal heads in a style which dates it to about 1100AD.

A chalice, still in use in the Catholic church in Cashel, has an inscription indicating that it was made for use in the cathedral in 1649. The Protestant archbishop, Thomas Fulwar, who died in 1667, bequeathed money for the manufacture of a new flagon, cup and paten for the cathedral and these survive with an inscription to that effect. Further church plate was donated by the wife of Archbishop Palliser in 1715.

Above: Bell crest,
Right: Cashel Crozier (National Museum of Ireland)

The Friary, Abbey and Town of Cashel

The Dominican Friary

The church, which is all that remains of the Dominican Friary, is situated on a back street between the Rock and the main street of Cashel. In medieval times it was immediately outside the walled town and within its own enclosure. It was founded by Archbishop David Ó Gilla Pátraic, who was probably also involved in building work at the cathedral.

The row of nine lancet windows in the south wall of the choir is typical of 13th-century Irish friaries. Other original features that survive are the plain west doorway and a row of windows at a high level in the north wall of the nave above the roof of the cloister walk, which, along with the domestic buildings would have been at this side of the church. A south transept was added in the later 13th century but the arches between the nave and the aisle and transept on this side have disappeared.

After an accidental fire around 1480 extensive restoration work was carried out by Archbishop John Cantwell. The tower between the nave and choir was probably added at this time and smaller traceried windows were inserted incongruously into the earlier blocked-up openings at the east end of the choir and south end of the transept. The friary was dissolved in 1540 and passed through the hands of various lay owners before being made a National Monument.

East window, Dominican Friary.

The Friary, Abbey and Town of Cashel

Hore Abbey

The remains of the last Cistercian abbey to be founded in medieval times in Ireland stand in fields
to the west of the Rock. Founded in 1272 by Archbishop David Mac Carvill as a daughter house of
Mellifont in Co. Louth, its name in Latin was *de Rupe* (of the rock). The modern name, attested
since the 16th century, is probably a translation from the Irish *An Mainistir Liath* (the grey abbey)
and should then be more correctly written hoar. The Cistercians were known as the Grey Monks from
the colour of their habits. The original building work was completed in the years immediately after
1272 and comprised of a cruciform church with two chapels in each transept and an aisled nave
with small quatrefoil windows above the nave arcade. The work is similar to, but plainer than, the
transepts and nave of the cathedral on the Rock. Putlog holes in the walls, to secure scaffolding
during construction, are now particularly noticeable in the ruined building.

The church suffered considerable alteration in the 15th century when blocking walls were inserted
cutting off most of the nave and the transepts and a tower was constructed over the old crossing.
The reduction in the size of the church appears to reflect a considerably smaller community in late
medieval times. The remaining west end of the nave was at that time, or in the post-dissolution
period, divided into three storeys of accommodation and the tall lancets at the west end were
divided into smaller windows with ogee heads. Uniquely among Irish Cistercian houses, the cloister
and domestic buildings were on the north side of the church but little now remains apart from the
east range, with its 13th-century projecting chapter house, which was altered at a later period. At
the Dissolution in 1541 only the abbot, Patrick Stackpool, and one monk were granted pensions,
though there is a mention also of three priests. By that time communities of such small numbers
were not unusual.

Hore Abbey

The Friary, Abbey and Town of Cashel

The town of Cashel and the Bolton Library

The town of Cashel was founded as a new town on the level ground to the south of the Rock by one of the archbishops sometime prior to 1218 when it was taken into the king's hands. This caused a protracted dispute between the archbishop and the Crown which lasted until 1228, when the town was restored to him. Archbishop Marianus Ua Briain granted a charter to Cashel in 1230. This was subsequently confirmed by Archbishop Roland Baron in 1557 and by a number of monarchs over the centuries. Charles I granted a charter in 1639 which gave it the status of a city. Cashel had defensive walls and substantial sections of them survive such as those on the south and east sides of the graveyard of St John's parish church. On the Main Street there is a heritage centre and a fine urban tower house, now part of a hotel, with a modern incongruous high-arched entrance, which makes it look like a gateway.

St John's parish church is on a narrow street running southwards from the Main Street. This 18th-century church, on the site of a medieval church, became the Church of Ireland cathedral in the mid 1700s when the cathedral on the Rock was abandoned. There are four very fine late 13th-century effigies set up against the town wall in the graveyard. Three are of women, one of these a member of the Hackett family, while the fourth is of a knight in chain mail and surcoat and holding a shield. All four are depicted with crossed legs. Also here is the Bolton Library (open to the public), which contains the library of Theophilus Bolton, Archbishop of Cashel (1730-44), and includes many early printed books. Between the Main Street and the Rock is the very fine archbishops' palace, built by Archbishop Bolton in 1730-2 to the design of Edward Lovett Pearce and now used as a hotel.

Cashel c. 1840 from Hall's Ireland.

Athassel Priory

The large priory of Canons Regular of St Augustine at Athassel on the River Suir about five miles from Cashel (via Golden) is a very impressive ruin covering some four acres (1.6ha). Remains of a large church with an aisled nave, transepts, Lady Chapel and a later crossing tower survive along with extensive remains of the cloister and domestic buildings, an enclosing wall, a gatehouse and bridge. Founded by William de Burgo about 1200AD, its possessions at the Dissolution included over 1000 acres (400ha) and the revenue from 45 rectories. Some fine medieval tomb sculpture survives including a 13th- or 14th-century grave slab with two incised figures and the tomb side carved with knights, which is now on display in the Hall of the Vicars Choral at Cashel.